COLLINS *Esse*

Effective Differentiation

Frances James and Kit Brown

Collins Educational
An imprint of HarperCollins*Publishers*

Published by Collins Educational
An imprint of HarperCollins*Publishers*
77-85 Fulham Palace Road
Hammersmith
London W6 8JB

First published 1998

ISBN 0 00 317722 X

Designed by Chi Leung
Printed by Martins the Printers Ltd, Berwick on Tweed

Contents

Introduction

Although it may seem that differentiation is something new, it is, in fact, what good teachers have always done – recognising that children in their class differ in many ways, and then planning and teaching lessons so that, despite these differences, all children make the best progress possible.

Differentiation has gained much greater attention recently for several reasons:

- The introduction of the National Curriculum has heightened teachers' awareness that there are children in each class who are working at different levels within the National Curriculum programmes of study.

- OFSTED inspections have reported on the lack of effective differentiation in some schools or the underachievement of specific groups of children in others. In the new OFSTED framework one of the criteria for judging the quality of teaching is *'the extent to which teachers employ methods and organisational strategies which match the curricular objectives and the needs of all pupils'*. Inspectors are expected to *'identify the level of challenge in the content, activities and learning resources provided for pupils with differing attainment'* and they should evaluate *'whether teaching is well matched to the pupils' stage of learning and moves them on'*.

- Since the 1981 Education Act there has been a move towards integrating pupils with a wide range of special educational needs into mainstream schools. This very positive movement has been reinforced by the recent Green Paper *Excellence for All Children*, which emphasises the move towards greater inclusion. It is, however, vital that these children are active participants in the class and not merely spectators. This requires class teachers to adopt teaching approaches which will ensure that being part of a mainstream school is a positive educational experience for the children and that they are able to learn and progress. It is equally important that the valuable presence of children with learning difficulties does not limit the progress that other children can make.

- The needs of more able children have received greater prominence. It is recognised that these children's learning needs to be extended to allow them to reach their full potential.

- Many teachers report that there is now greater expectation from parents for schools to organise learning in ways that meet their children's individual needs and strengths. It could be argued that this has arisen from greater public awareness about education through the publication of OFSTED reports, league tables and general press attention. Reporting children's attainment to parents at the end of Key Stages may also have heightened awareness.

How do children differ?

As in the OFSTED framework, the focus on children's differences tends to be on their different ability or levels of attainment. These factors will have the greatest impact in the classroom, but to gain a broader perspective about differentiation it is valuable to think about the variety of ways in which children differ:

- age and emotional maturity
- gender
- socio-economic background
- ethnic and/or religious background
- previous educational and home experiences.

All these factors can have an influence on the child's performance in the classroom.

Differences in children's ability

'Ability' is a very broad term. There are children who are of overall high or low ability, but most children will have areas of particular cognitive strength or weakness. It is helpful to analyse the children's cognitive abilities in slightly finer detail.

The areas of ability that have particular significance for academic achievement are:

- **linguistic ability** – the child's ability to understand language (receptive language) and their ability to express their ideas (expressive language). There are a significant number of children in schools for whom English is an additional language and their needs will need particular consideration.

- **spatial ability** – the ability to recognise and position objects in space. (This has an impact on children's mathematical achievement and other areas of the curriculum – correct orientation is necessary to be able to recognise and write letters correctly.)

- **short- and long-term memory** – this is fundamental to learning as it allows children to retain information. Children with specific learning difficulties, for example dyslexia, frequently have problems with their auditory short-term memory. When learning to read children have to be able to retain information in their short-term working memory before committing the information to their long-term memory store.

- **concentration** – the ability to sustain concentration during a task and to avoid distractions.

Children also have different skills. The skills that will play the most significant part in the child's learning are:

- **literacy skills** – some children have significant difficulty in learning to read and/or spell. The difficulties in learning to read may relate to decoding or recognising words. There are also children who, although they decode accurately, have poor comprehension skills and find it difficult to extract meaning from print. As so much of the curriculum is taught using the written word and requires the children to write to record their work, the work for some children has to be differentiated to accommodate these difficulties.

- **numeracy skills**
- **motor skills** – these include fine and gross motor skills.
- **organisational skills** – these can have an impact on the children's overall study skills. Are they able to organise their work space, to sequence their work and to develop strategies for approaching their work?

To differentiate work for children you will need to take into consideration these various abilities and skills of the children. Ways in which you can assess children's abilities are addressed in Chapter 5.

Differentiation by task and by outcome

Differentiation is often spoken about in terms of two main approaches – differentiation by task or by outcome. Both these approaches are valid and can be highly effective. They both rely on accurate assessment information about the children.

When differentiating by task the teacher recognises the different ability and/or skill levels of children and then plans different tasks, within a common theme, for the children to do. To differentiate by task you will need to know what the children can currently do, understand and know, to enable you to plan appropriate tasks.

When differentiating by outcome all the children do the same task but the teacher expects different products from the children, reflecting their different abilities. It is vital to know what is an acceptable outcome for individual children; three lines of writing from one child may be a considerable achievement and represent good progress, whereas three pages from another child may be an underachievement.

Other approaches to differentiation

In addition to differentiation by task and by outcome, there are other ways in which you can recognise the differences between children through your planning and teaching. These include:

- using different teaching styles
- having different expectations of the pace at which

different children will complete tasks

- being sensitive to the children's different language abilities
- changing the classroom organisation
- providing different resources (including different reading material)
- allowing the children different ways to record their work
- giving children different levels and types of feedback and reinforcement
- using information technology.

In this book we have described these approaches in some detail, providing practical ideas and approaches for differentiated teaching.

Teaching styles

Every teacher has a preferred teaching style, the one with which they feel most comfortable. There is no one style which is more appropriate for employing differentiation techniques and, in fact, altering your teaching style is one way of differentiating, recognising that children have different learning styles. The vital thing is to adopt a teaching style for a lesson that is the most appropriate to ensure that all children will gain as much as they can from that lesson.

Interactive whole class teaching

This approach involves a high level of interaction between you and the children. This may include the children answering questions or coming to the front of the class to demonstrate something. By definition all the children should be involved, therefore you will need to ensure that the questions that you ask and the demands that you make will address the different ability levels within the class.

In the example opposite, reference to groups does not mean that the children are sitting or working in groups – it reflects the children's current level of understanding in number.

There are certain things to consider when organising the classroom for whole class teaching. Check that children who are easily distracted are sitting close to you and not on the fringe of the class, and that children who have poor hearing or eyesight are well placed to hear and see everything that is going on.

Children working independently

This approach is appropriate for all children. Children with learning difficulties often find it difficult to concentrate and are easily distracted. They can find it hard to work in the busy hum of a classroom. More able pupils need to learn to work independently and to develop a good working pace.

Example

Subject: Maths

Central learning objective: To count in twos to 50

Resources: Overhead Projector and number square (5 x 10)

Classroom organisation: All children facing screen

Activities:

1 Quick fire counting to 50, children taking it in turns to say numbers. (Ask James and Fiona to say some numbers between 40 and 50 to check that they are secure with these.)

2 Children to come up to OHP and count on in twos and shade in number. (Start with green group, as this will reinforce their current understanding.)

3 Ask children to describe resulting pattern.

4 Children take it in turns to read out the shaded numbers (ask one of green group to say what they have counted in).

5 Turn off OHP; children to count in twos as a class and then in turns (concentrate on blue and green groups).

To follow up this whole class activity you may wish to differentiate the tasks.

- James and Fiona to fill in number square and then shade in pattern of twos.
- Green group to write number pattern in twos.
- Blue group to explore the characteristics of odd and even numbers using number square.

If children are working independently it is likely that you will be differentiating mainly through the resources that you make available to them and the amount of time that you spend with individuals. The resources which you provide should be readily accessible to the children; they should be able to get the support materials that they need without having to ask you.

Every classroom presents certain physical constraints which restrict your flexibility in changing the arrangement of the furniture. If you are expecting children to work independently it is desirable, if not always possible, for the children to sit separately. If they sit in groups they will be tempted to try to work and talk as a group. Remember that if you are expecting the children to look at writing on a central board they should be sitting so that they can see it with relative ease.

Independent working often requires the children to use study skills. Children's abilities to undertake independent study will vary. This must be recognised in your planning and teaching.

You need to consider the children's:

- literacy levels
- knowledge of alphabetical order
- skill in using contents pages, indexes, etc.
- ability to skim read

- note-taking skills
- ability to identify important information
- organisational skills.

Although you will be planning specific lessons to develop these areas in all the children, you will need to accommodate the differences when the children are undertaking independent research:

- Make sure that you have a good range of reference materials available for the children. Include books that require different levels of literacy skills – some with a limited text, some with clear layout, some that incorporate pictures in the index, some that will extend the more able pupils, etc. If suitable materials are not available you may have to make a reference sheet which will be accessible for certain children.

- Children with poor organisational skills may need the support of a task list (see page 40). You may need to provide some children with an equipment list to help them organise themselves.

- For children who have difficulty taking notes or identifying the relevant information from a text, provide a sheet to help them structure their investigation.

Example

Daily life in Ancient Greece

Ancient Greeks wore

They lived in

They grew

They drank

They enjoyed

Working in a group

The reason for working in a group needs to be clearly defined. Sometimes children sit in a group but do not actually work as a group – this has more to do with classroom organisation than choosing the relevant teaching style for the activity.

For some learning tasks it is highly appropriate for the children to work in a group, and children need to learn to work collaboratively. Children with learning difficulties often respond well to working in a group or in a pair. Working with others gives them confidence, as they can check out their answers with their friends before having to commit them to paper or tell the teacher.

There are different ways of deciding the composition of groups:

- friendship groups
- groups based on the ability particularly relevant to the activity
- general ability groups, based on ability not directly related to the activity
- mixed ability groups
- groups based on age.

Again, the arrangement that you choose will depend upon what you want the children to learn. Friendship groups are appropriate for activities that require a high level of co-operation (drama, etc.), ability groupings when you plan to differentiate by task, mixed ability groups when there are elements of the task to which children can contribute different skills, and groupings based on age are relevant when you have a mixed age class and wish to cover different aspects of the National Curriculum.

Using mixed ability groups requires particularly careful planning. It is important that all the children in the group feel that they are able to make a valuable contribution and that they will learn from the activity. There should be no 'passengers', and you do not want the progress of the more able pupils to be limited because they are having to act as mini-teachers all the time. Equally, you do not want the lower ability children to lose confidence.

When planning such an activity analyse the elements involved. Consider the composition of the group and decide which child would be able to contribute to each element. It is necessary to build on the children's strengths; for example some will have stronger verbal skills, recording skills or graphic skills.

Example

Subject: Science (Key Stage 2)

Central learning objective: To know that sounds get fainter as they travel away from sources.

Activity: Children to take a variety of sound sources into playground and to measure the distance at which they can no longer hear the different sounds.

All children take part in the experiment but within the task they have specific roles:

Carlton – group organiser, to ensure that it is a 'fair test'
Liza – to record results
Shaun – to co-ordinate measuring
Francis – to take responsibility for equipment.

Follow-up:
Carlton – to write brief summary of what they did
Liza – to record results on computer
Shaun – to represent what they did pictorially
Francis – to prepare short verbal report for whole class.

Experiential learning

Children learn from doing, and experiential learning activities can be particularly potent for children who find it more difficult to understand abstract concepts. (It is a good technique to start many types of lessons with a practical element, allowing children to experiment and demonstrate aspects of the learning objective.)

Lessons that involve experiential learning, however, require a tight structure with clear aims and objectives. Children need guidance and instruction, and less able children will require particular support. Without such structure it is highly likely that the children will not discover what you intend them to, nor will they consolidate skills and understanding.

Determine the central learning objective and the type of support that individual children or groups may need. Ensure that your planning incorporates sufficient challenge for more able pupils. Identify the types of resources that the children will need to complete the activity successfully.

Example

Subject: Art

Central Learning Objective: To know that by mixing certain colours you can make different colours. Children to be able to say three different colour combinations.

Resources:

Group 1	colour palettes with three primary colours grid for recording findings
Group 2	colour palettes with six colours grid for recording findings
Group 3	colour palettes with six colours paper for making grid to record findings

Grids used:

Group 1

	and		make	
	and		make	
	and		make	

Use paints to show results

Group 2

	and		make	

Use words to show results

One aspect of experiential learning is the use of drama and role play. This can be an effective way of involving children in learning activities. Such approaches work well for introducing children to more complex information or concepts, such as the sequence or content of certain historical events, demonstrating division by children sharing things out, showing how people change as they grow older, etc.

When planning, take into account the different levels of emotional maturity that the children might have, their confidence in speaking in front of others, etc. Some children might find the exercise very daunting, and should be included in a slightly less prominent role. These children may be more comfortable working in a pair.

Working with other adults in the classroom

Having another adult in the classroom allows greater flexibility and can enhance the opportunities for differentiation. The other adult may be a teacher, support assistant or volunteer, possibly a parent helper. Careful planning is necessary to make maximum use of the opportunities of having an extra adult in the classroom present.

Using another teacher in the classroom

Your colleague may be a support teacher who is working with children with specific difficulties, or your school may organise its staffing to give teachers the chance of team teaching for specific lessons.

If your colleague is a support teacher there are several ways in which you can organise the lesson to meet the children's needs.

- The support teacher works with a designated group of children with learning difficulties, supporting them in reaching the central learning objective for the whole class.

- The support teacher works on specific skills with a group of children, either in the class or by withdrawing them.

- The support teacher withdraws a group of children for either pre- or post-lesson tutoring; in other words, they either prepare the children for a forthcoming lesson, introducing them to key concepts and vocabulary, or check the children's understanding and knowledge once the lesson has taken place.

- The support teacher works with a group of more able children to extend their skills and knowledge.

- You and the support teacher team teach.

- The class is divided into two 'halves', allowing more time and attention for all children.

- The support teacher takes responsibility for most of the class, while you work intensively with a group of children.

- The support teacher works outside the classroom preparing appropriate resources to help specific children gain access to forthcoming lessons.

The choice of which approach you adopt will depend on:

- the content of the lesson (for example, the support teacher could prepare resources while the class watches a video)
- the teaching style used
- the skills and interests of the two teachers involved
- the needs of the children.

All these approaches require joint planning. The following issues need to be included in this planning.

- If your colleague is going to work in the classroom helping a group of children to achieve the central learning objective, they will obviously need to know what that objective is in order to plan which particular strategies and resources they will need to employ.

- If the support teacher is going to withdraw a group of children to work on specific skills, which are frequently literacy skills, it is important that your colleague knows the approach used in the school for developing the skills so that the work is complementary. It is also useful if the support teacher knows the content of the lesson in the main classroom; if at all possible, links should be made between the work of the class and the withdrawal group.

- In team teaching it is necessary to define the roles of the different members of staff. These include not only the delivery of the lesson but also roles and responsibilities for managing children's behaviour.

Working with a support assistant in the classroom

Support assistants provide invaluable support in the classroom. As they are working under your direction it is necessary for them to be given clear instructions about the role that you want them to play. They should not have the sole responsibility for planning specific teaching activities. When you are planning the work with the support assistant it is important that you describe the areas of learning and language that are a high priority for individual children. It is very helpful if all the relevant planning information is recorded on a sheet which is handed to the support assistant before the lesson starts.

Ways of using a support assistant include:

- The assistant works with a designated group of children, supporting them towards the central learning objective.
- The assistant makes differentiated resources for use with the class.

Working with volunteers in the classroom

Many primary classrooms benefit from the assistance of parental volunteers. The traditional use of volunteers is to hear children read – remember to let children with very good literacy skills read to volunteers as well as those who have weaker reading skills.

There are, however, other ways in which you can use their services:

- Ask volunteers to read or tell stories to children who have poor language skills. Interactive story-telling, when the reader involves the child in the story by asking them questions, has been shown to have a very positive impact on the development of children's vocabulary. Being able to read a story to an individual child is a luxury for which teachers can rarely find the time. Run short training sessions for volunteers to show them how to get the most out of sessions. If parents are hearing children read, training sessions will also be needed. Simple advice booklets can be very useful.

- Use volunteers to run group reading sessions. These are particularly useful in stimulating more sophisticated responses to literature in able children. Identify a group reader which will extend the children's response, and provide the volunteer with a prompt sheet of questions or comments which will generate a discussion. Volunteers can also supervise play readings. These may be extended by allowing the children to enact the plays, taking different responsibilities for acting, directing, checking the accuracy of the reading, etc.

- Establish a parents' workshop for making resources that will help you to differentiate the curriculum. It is a good idea to identify a specific day every month (for example, the last Tuesday in each month) when the workshop takes place. This will help you to organise the workshop, by writing your shopping list and gathering together the materials that the volunteers will need.

Teacher behaviour

One of the commonest forms of differentiation is the level of teacher intervention with individual children or groups of children. By providing different levels and kinds of support, teachers recognise the different needs of the children.

This form of differentiation is used in all forms of teaching. In whole class teaching, teachers can differentiate by their questioning techniques – extending and challenging the more able pupils, while checking that the less able children have understood and also offering them appropriate challenges. If the children are working in groups the amount of time that teachers spend with groups may vary, depending on what stage the children have reached.

Children in your class have a right to equal access to your time. It is tempting to let more able children proceed at their own pace as they are able to work without so much of your assistance. It may be that in a particular lesson it is appropriate that one group does not receive as much of your attention as others, but you need to ensure that over the week all the children have an equal share of your teaching time.

Teachers often comment that they spend a disproportionate amount of time with children who find learning more difficult. This may not be the most effective use of the teacher's time. It is important to anticipate these children's needs and plan when it would be most appropriate to intervene. Instead of having to spend one long interval of time with the group when they are well and truly 'stuck', consider whether it would be better to:

- check that the group or individual has fully understood your instructions just after you have delivered them

- visit the group at regular but brief intervals, checking that they are still are on task and giving them feedback on the work that they have done so far

- give them shorter learning targets and ask them to tell you when they have finished each element.

Children with learning difficulties need to learn to work independently and also to experience tasks with which they feel successful. It is therefore important occasionally to give them tasks which will allow them to work on their own without relying on you. These activities reinforce skills, and develop the children's fluency and accuracy with specific skills.

With more able pupils, who are able to sustain concentration for longer periods of time, it can be appropriate to spend a more concentrated period of time with them – setting the task in a more sophisticated context, presenting different resources, challenging their responses and asking them to expand their answers.

Levels of reinforcement and feedback

It is important that all children receive accurate feedback and praise about their work. Children want to hear that their work is good, but this reinforcement becomes more powerful if they are told why the work has been praised. This allows them to repeat the successful aspects of their work and develop the areas that require refinement. This feedback should be differentiated depending on the children's ability.

If children are encountering particular difficulty with an area of learning, draw up a target sheet on which they can record their achievements.

Remember to praise and give feedback to the more able children, as well as to those who find learning more difficult! This may seem an obvious remark but it is quite easy to slip into presuming that they will always produce work of a high standard and take this for granted. If their work is not accorded the recognition that it deserves they may lose motivation. Discuss the aspects of their work that you particularly like.

You should differentiate your feedback and reinforcement to children with emotional and behavioural difficulties – those who are withdrawn as well as those who engage in low-level disruption. To encourage appropriate behaviour in such children, give them regular feedback about when they are behaving well. Most children know how to conform to classroom routines and established practices, but some do not. When you observe them working well, sharing things, etc., say, 'Well done, Susan, I am pleased to see you working hard'.

For children who are prone to high-level disruption, it is a good idea to draw up a specific chart for recording the behaviour that you wish to see.

Example

Andrew's playground chart — playing and sharing with other children nicely

	Morning	Lunch	Afternoon
Monday			
Tuesday			
Wednesday			
Thursday			
Friday			

Children who have behaviour difficulties respond particularly well to letters or notes homes describing their good behaviour.

Remember that children respond to different forms of praise. Many appreciate public recognition and will enjoy praise in front of the whole class. Other children find this difficult to accept. They need a more private form of recognition – a quiet word of praise, a smiley face in their book, or a private 'thumbs up'.

One way to show recognition of children's work is to display it in the classroom. It is important that the work of all the children is represented – this can present difficulties as some children's work may not reflect the standard you would wish, even though it may be a considerable achievement for those individual children.This can be addressed by using captions to annotate the work. For example:

I like Sasha's drawing – she remembered to draw the woman's arms.

Joe worked very hard to make sure that all his sums were right.

Classroom organisation

The organisation of the classroom supports the differentiated teaching approaches that you adopt and also the needs of individual children.

Seating arrangements

The organisation of the class will depend largely upon the teaching style that you have chosen to use and the nature of the activity. You must ask yourself whether the organisation of the classroom complements your teaching approach. The flexibility at your disposal will be determined by factors such as the size of the classroom, the type of furniture, etc.

For interactive whole class teaching all the children must be able to see you and any audio-visual aids (for example, a white board or overhead projector) that you are using. In practice this means that the children should be facing the front – any child having to turn round to see the board will be at a disadvantage. This approach to classroom organisation is also appropriate when you want the children to work independently and quietly, or even silently.

If children are working in a group, tables can be joined together to give the group an identity.

Practically, it is not possible to keep changing the classroom into many different variations, but some teachers have designed two, or maybe three, different arrangements. They have then taught the children to move the furniture, with minimal fuss and bother.

Meeting the needs of individual children

- If there are children with some kind of sensory impairment in your class, careful consideration should be given to where they sit. Children with a visual impairment will usually need to sit close to the front of the class with a good light source behind them. Children with hearing impairments who depend, to some extent, on lip reading need to sit where they have clear sight of the teacher and where the light enhances their view. If you are organising a class or group discussion, remember that some of the hearing-impaired children will need to look at the contributors and will miss much if children are talking behind them.

- Children with emotional and behavioural difficulties, particularly those who have difficulty concentrating, should sit in the heart of the class, not near a window or door where they can find even more sources of potential distraction.

Assessment and planning

Assessment is one of the keys to effective differentiated teaching.

Having clear assessment information about children's strengths and weaknesses allows you to plan in a way which recognises their differences, building on what they know and can do. Assessment should also be an integral part of teaching as it informs the next steps and enables you to evaluate the lesson.

The relationship between assessment, planning and teaching should be seen as a continuous cycle.

There are different types of assessment that can be used to inform your planning and teaching. With all forms of assessment it is vital to recognise children's strengths as well as any weaknesses. These strengths can play an important part in planning and teaching.

- **Standardised assessment (or norm-referenced)** – allows you to compare a pupil's achievement with a 'standard' population. The most common types of standardised assessments are reading and spelling tests. They give the children's performance in a variety of forms, for example a reading age, a standard score or a percentile.

  Standardised results will not tell you what to teach next but will highlight particular strengths and weaknesses that a child may have. For example, if a child has a reading age much lower than the majority of the class you will know that without some kind of additional support they will probably not be able to read worksheets that you have prepared.

  Standardised results can also alter your expectations of a child. Some children mask their abilities and are content with producing adequate work. Information about the child's underlying cognitive abilities (verbal and/or non-verbal) will expose their under-achievement.

Many schools use standardised assessments to screen children's reading skills at regular intervals, and schools are increasingly adopting screening procedures for assessing children's more general abilities, therefore this information will be available to all teachers. If, however, you are interested in a particular child's abilities, tests that you could use include:

- British Picture Vocabulary Scale – gives an indication of the child's understanding of vocabulary and has a good correlation with general intelligence
- Cognitive Abilities Test – measures verbal and non-verbal reasoning ability.

- **Criterion-referenced assessment** – tells you what the child can do. This is the most useful form of assessment for planning the next teaching steps, and is the core of teacher assessment.

  Examples of criterion-referenced assessment are:
  - the child knows 14/26 initial letter sounds
  - the child can read 8/12 most common keywords
  - the child can cut with scissors
  - the child can name the main external parts of the body, except 'elbow'.

  The level descriptors in the National Curriculum are criterion-referenced.

- **Observation** – is an underused form of assessment that provides valuable information about how children approach tasks, their preferred learning styles, with whom they work best and their study skills. It is often difficult in a busy classroom to undertake a lengthy observation, but it is well worth stepping back for two or three minutes to observe certain children. If you are fortunate enough to have a supporting member of staff in the classroom occasionally, ask them to observe the children working on specific tasks.

- **Children's self-assessment** – is another form of

assessment which is not always fully utilised. It is not necessary to conduct formal interviews; the children will tell you what they find easy or difficult, what resources they find useful or necessary, and the classroom organisation which they find the most conducive to learning.

A few extracts from pupil interviews are given here.

I like to find the reason for things ... In maths I prefer investigational work as opposed to book work because I find that much more interesting and gives you far more freedom of what you've got to do. I like to work when you've got general freedom of what you do – like you plan it out yourself and do things yourself. In English some of the things I don't like, like we read some stories that I don't find that interesting because the books that we read from are not the kind of book I normally read from and that I get enjoyment from reading. In music the sort of thing I do is quite a lot faster than the stuff we do here. We do quite basic stuff here. (Maria – a Year 6 pupil of above-average ability with particular musical talent)

I prefer to work individually on things like stories and stuff. Sometimes I am distracted because I try to explain things when people don't understand – like my ideas, I try to explain things like that. (Susan – a Year 5 pupil with learning difficulties who sits with a 'low-ability' group in the classroom)

I find it hard to organise myself. I tend to figure out what I'm going to do and just forget. Michael happens to be my friend – we sit together and work together. We talk a lot. I would probably get more done if I worked on my own. (John – a Year 4 pupil felt to be underachieving by his teacher)

It is clear that these extracts contain important information that would inform the planning of lessons and also the organisation of the classroom. Involving children in their own learning has an important impact on their attainment.

This range of assessment information about individual children will feed into lesson planning.

Planning differentiated lessons

Children are taught in a class and not on discrete individual programmes, except in very specific circumstances. There is tremendous value in learning as a member of a group, whichever teaching approach is used, be it whole class teaching, group work or experiential learning. When planning a lesson it is vital to identify the central learning objective for all pupils. This is the knowledge, skill and/or concept that you want all pupils to achieve by the end of the lesson or series of lessons. It will form the basis for your assessment at the end of the lesson.

What are the features of an appropriate central learning objective?

- It should be something which is key to the children's understanding of the subject, not something peripheral.

- It should be a realistic objective for the pupils but one that sets high expectations.

Obviously some children will reach the central learning objective in small steps and will then need chances to rehearse and reinforce it. Other children will achieve it comparatively easily and for them you will need to plan opportunities to use this objective as a springboard for extension activities. (The assessment data you have from previous lessons will allow you to anticipate which pupils will require which learning opportunities – but be prepared to be surprised! Some children may find a specific concept easier or more challenging than you anticipated.)

An example of this approach to lesson planning is given on the following page. With such a lesson scheme you can plan a common lesson introduction – introducing the key vocabulary, asking all the children to name the shapes and to identify the key difference between two-dimensional and three-dimensional shapes.

Schools have adopted a variety of forms for lesson planning. It is important that you use one that you feel comfortable with, and

Example

Key Stage 1 Maths: Shape, Space and Measure.

Central learning objective: To make a cube from a net

Group 1
- Sort 2D/3D shapes (reinforcement)
- Identify difference – use word 'solid' (reinforcement)
- Name shapes – square, rectangle, circle, cube, sphere (reinforcement)
- Using pre-prepared net, make cube

- Name shape of cube faces (possible extension)

Group 2
- Using pre-prepared net, make cube
- Name shape of cube faces
- Fill in worksheet (number of faces/corners/edges)
- Use square shapes to model a cube net

- Draw a net to make a bigger cube (possible extension)

that it contains all the information that you need but does not require endless form-filling for the sake of it.

One suggested format for lesson planning is given on the following page. It is designed to be flexible – you can change the number of groups; in some cases, you may wish to identify specific learning steps for individual pupils or you may plan one set of learning steps for all pupils and differentiate by outcome (see below). Some teachers find it useful to include the key vocabulary and a space for describing the common introduction to the lesson.

It is important that the lesson plan focuses on learning objectives and not solely on the activities. It is only by identifying the objectives for the lesson that you will be able to determine what the children have learnt.

Lesson plan(s)

Subject: **Date(s):**

Central learning objective

Group 1*   Group 2   Group 3

* write children's names if not fixed groups

-
-
-
-

Assessment notes/evaluation

Resources/materials

This approach involves planning different tasks aimed to allow all pupils to reach the central learning objective. It is possible to incorporate the idea of a central learning objective but differentiate by outcome. Using this approach you identify the central learning objective for all the children but, using your knowledge of the children based on previous assessment, you will expect different levels of understanding, depth or pace for completing the task from different children and/or provide different resources to help them finish the task successfully.

Example

Central learning objective: Accurate use of full stops.

Activity: Written account of visit from community police officer

Time available: 40 minutes
Expectations:

Group 1: Two completed accurate sentences (use of word lists)

Group 2: Half page of work – accurate sentences (use of word books)

Group 3: Page of work – accurate sentences (use of dictionaries)

These are minimum expectations, based on your knowledge of the children. You would obviously encourage the children to perform beyond these expectations. It is important to tell the children what you are expecting from them before they start. Targets should be shared with the children.

If you want to differentiate by pace, the expectations might be the same for all the children but you would allow different children or groups different lengths of time to complete the task.

Planning assessment opportunities

To complete the assessment–planning–teaching cycle you need to ensure that within the lesson you are able to determine different children's attainment. (It will obviously help if you have identified a central learning objective as this becomes one of your benchmarks.) Ways of assessing the children's achievement include observation during the lesson, looking at their work when they have finished it and talking to the children.

Of course, children may be able to do something at the end of the lesson but forget the skill after that. Unfortunately you cannot guarantee that children remember things! At the end of a topic you may find it useful to assess the children's retention of the key concepts and knowledge. If you want to make a summative assessment make sure that the type of assessment that you use allows all the children to show the full extent of their knowledge.

For some children it is necessary to differentiate your approaches to assessment. Children with weak literacy skills may not have the writing skills to write down what they know or understand. With these children you will need to think of other ways of assessing their knowledge and understanding. This could be by questioning them, or by asking them to draw pictures or to record their answers on tape.

One aspect that can be incorporated into the teaching/planning cycle is the evaluation of the lesson. This evaluation will inform your future planning, allowing you to identify which teaching strategies worked and should be repeated and which did not achieve the desired outcomes.

As time is such a precious commodity it is also important to consider the time that it took you to prepare the lesson and the associated materials, in order to assess whether the session was 'cost-effective'. In other words, was the time investment that you made matched in the gains that the children made in their learning?

Several questions will inform your evaluation:

- Did all the children achieve the central learning objective?

- Did some children rely on you too heavily? For example, were they constantly asking for clarification?

- Were all the children working purposefully during the lesson? (Any signs of low-level disruption might be an indication that either more able children were insufficiently challenged or less able children found the work inaccessible.)

- What was the standard of presentation of the children's work? (Poorly presented work may indicate that the children were not engaged with the activity.)
- Did the children enjoy the lesson?
- Did you enjoy the lesson?

A pertinent question that you should ask after a period of time has elapsed is 'Did the children retain the central learning objective?'

To help you answer the questions there are various sources of evidence:

- the children's work
- observation during the lesson – if you have a supporting member of staff in the class you can ask them to contribute to these observations
- talking to the children about what aspects of the lesson they enjoyed
- reflecting on how you felt at the end of the lesson.

The answers to the questions may indicate that you felt that certain groups or individual children had achieved well but that others had not. This is valuable information and will provide a good basis for planning the next series of lessons.

Learning resources

The provision of appropriate learning resources is one of the most effective and commonly used approaches to differentiation. A child with weaker mathematical skills said in an interview that she found that maths was particularly hard in her new class because she was no longer allowed to use bricks to help her do her sums. This is a simple but rather striking example of how children's learning can be supported by providing the appropriate resources.

Classrooms will have a variety of available resources which range from basic materials to allow children to complete their work (paper, pencils, etc.) to resources which illustrate or support the acquisition of knowledge and concepts.

Basic classroom equipment

Furniture

Classroom furniture should be chosen taking into account differences in the children's physical maturity and development. Children grow at different rates, and the height of standard classroom chairs and tables may mean that some children are working in uncomfortable positions, with poor posture. There are a few children who find working on a horizontal surface very difficult and will produce work of a much higher standard if they work on a slanting surface. These angled boards are often appropriate for left-handed children.

Writing implements

Children will have different levels of fine motor control. It is important that there are a range of writing implements to accommodate these different skills. Children with poorer fine motor skills often write better if they use a thicker pencil – some children may need a special pencil grip attachment. Children who have developed a good fluent writing style should be allowed to experiment with a range of writing implements.

Pay particular attention to the needs of left-handed children. It is important that the school has a supply of left-handed scissors and other specifically adapted resources.

Paper

A variety of sizes of paper should be available within the class. Children with weaker literacy skills can be daunted when presented with what seems like a large piece of paper to fill. Give these children smaller pieces of paper or paper that has some space already filled, for example with a picture or pattern. However, some children with literacy difficulties have large writing and need more space.

It is now recognised that some children and adults find using white paper for reading or writing uncomfortable as it generates a glare. Some children have reported that black print on white paper appears to move. It is a good idea to provide a range of pastel-coloured paper for the children to choose from – they will choose the paper that they find the most comfortable.

Rulers

The use of rulers can present serious problems for some children. It is important to have a range of rulers available. Children who do have difficulty need to use rulers which are very clear and use the minimum amount of relevant information – possibly using only centimetres. You will want more able children to achieve a greater accuracy with their measuring, and they should be provided with more detailed rulers.

A simple way of differentiating for children who have difficulty in controlling the positioning of rulers is to give them a small piece of Blu-Tak to secure the ruler to the table surface.

Mathematical equipment

Mathematics is a particularly abstract subject; it is necessary to provide children who have more difficulty with abstract concepts with a range of practical materials to illustrate the concept that you are teaching. These children are also likely to find it more difficult to generalise their learning or to make analogies. You can help them achieve this by providing a number of different examples. For example, children with a good understanding of the qualities of shape and space will quickly make the generalisation that two-dimensional figures with three sides are all triangles – they can progress to investigate other features of triangles or different shapes. Other children will need to experience many examples before they make the generalisation about three-sided figures.

Ways of storing work

Children should be given increasing responsibility for storing their work. Children with good organisational skills should be encouraged to develop them. This can be promoted by providing them with files and by teaching them how to order their work. Children with weaker organisational skills require more structure and may need to continue using exercise books.

Children with poor organisational skills often forget basic working equipment; this leads to them starting their work late. You can differentiate your approach with these children by:

- keeping a stock of spare basic equipment in the class for them to borrow
- providing them with a checklist of equipment to which they are expected to refer
- making sure that they keep their equipment in the class.

More able children should be encouraged to take responsibility for their own equipment, and they will respond to having open access to general classroom resources.

General learning resources

Having a wide range of learning resources available allows for differentiated support for learning.

Children with learning difficulties find abstract concepts more challenging and so respond well to practical, 'concrete' resources which illustrate the concept, as described in the section on mathematical equipment. These children frequently need to see and witness what you are endeavouring to convey.

Examples of such resources include:

- artefacts (including things from children's everyday

experience)
- photographs
- pictures
- videos
- models.

More able children need to have experience of these resources too, but they should also be provided with more abstract materials which let them extend their understanding.

For children with different cultural or ethnic backgrounds, endeavour to include resources or artefacts which come from their cultural heritage or present. If English is their second language seek resources which are presented in their mother tongue.

The concepts that children with learning difficulties find problematical are often fundamental to the understanding of a subject. A good example of this is the concept of time which underlies the understanding of history. Some children's concept of time barely extends to yesterday and the idea of generations or centuries past offers considerable challenge. Introducing a time line can help the children to develop an understanding of time. It will be necessary to limit the time line for some children to aspects of their own life and then gradually add events from their family's life. You will be able to use a more complex time line which incorporates aspects beyond living memory for children with a more sophisticated appreciation of time.

The idea of difference between life now and in times past is best illustrated when the children can see examples of what you wish them to compare rather than having to rely on verbal or written description. More able children respond well to a mixture of resources.

7 *Language*

Language is fundamental to learning. A child's ability to understand language and to express their ideas has a profound impact on their success in the classroom. Children have very different language abilities, and it is important that these differences are recognised and accommodated in teaching and planning.

Various aspects of language need to be considered: the language of everyday interaction, the language of instruction, and subject-specific language. It is vital that teachers provide a good language model for children, but be aware that some children may not understand certain words and concepts, which as teachers and adults we take for granted. A wonderful example is found in *Cider with Rosie* by Laurie Lee. On his first day at school Laurie is asked by the teacher to 'wait here for the present'. When he returns home he tells his mother that he waited and waited but the present never came. It is an informative, and often salutary, exercise to tape parts of your lessons and then analyse the language that you used.

When instructing children you can recognise the differences in their language abilities by using various strategies. (Some children's difficulties may relate not just to language but also to their memory capacity.)

- When you have introduced a lesson, check that individual pupils or groups of children have understood what you have said by asking them to repeat it. This exercise can be very informative; many children are reluctant to ask for clarification of instructions or specific words. If they use words that might be new to them, ask them to explain what they think the words mean.

- Provide some children with a simple task list or summary which they can refer to as they work through the task:

- Group the children in mixed ability groups. Give a linguistically able child the task of recapping the introduction to the rest of the group. (Try to listen to check that they are correctly reporting your words!)

- At the end of the lesson ask the children with restricted language to report what they did, using the appropriate language. This will help them to remember new or unfamiliar language.

- Encourage linguistically more able children to use synonyms.

Subject-specific language

Some subject-specific language may seem to be common currency, and there is a natural presumption that the children understand it. It is not, for example, that unusual to find children in years 2 and 3 who still do not understand the difference between a word and a letter. They may give the appearance of knowing the difference by using the words, but it is important to check that they have a true understanding as any confusion will seriously impede their progress in reading.

When introducing a lesson identify the language that is central to the children's understanding, and then bring in other words which will extend the more able children. To meet the different children's language levels it is possible to introduce and reinforce the words in different ways. An example that illustrates some of these methods in a Geographical context is given on pages 43 and 44.

- Write the words on a board as you say them. In recognition of the different literacy levels of the pupils ask some children to read out the words as you write them. Next demonstrate to all the children good ways of decoding the words (for example: highlight the initial letter sounds; show them how to break the word up into syllables; highlight particular letter strings; remind them of words that look the same and share the same spelling patterns; encourage them to look for smaller words within the words). When you have completed the list ask other children to read through the words to reinforce them. If you have children with very weak literacy skills you may draw a quick picture by the side of the word to act as a visual prompt (Glossary 1).

- Provide glossaries for the children to refer to as they work (Glossary 2). These can be differentiated in the level of sophistication and the amount of written language that you use. Some children may use these predominantly as spelling lists, others as sources of information to inform their work.

- Give more able children a list of the words and ask them to find the definitions; the list can then be used as a glossary (Glossary 3). Or you can make the task even more open-ended – ask the children to decide which are the important words and to write them down on a separate piece of paper and find the definitions.

- Encourage all the children to use a variety of reference sources. Provide different support materials in recognition of the children's different literacy levels and general abilities, for example, books which demand different literacy skills, CD-ROMs, etc.

Subject: *Geography*

Topic: Comparison – rural/urban area

Key vocabulary: farm, field, village, shop, supermarket, road, motorway, countryside, town, city, factories, offices

Extension vocabulary: housing estates, rural, urban, pollution

---

Glossary 1

Words   you   may   need:

Town   and   country   field   shop

farm   countryside   town   factories

Glossary 2

Town and country

Words that you may need:

rural – the countryside

urban – towns or cities

housing estates – groups of houses which were built at the same time

factories – where things are made

etc.

Glossary 3

Town and country

You will need these words.
Write down what they mean, or draw a picture.

farm

field

factories

etc.

(Include other words, as appropriate, that will challenge more able pupils.)

Using texts

In the primary classroom texts are used for two main purposes – to develop the children's reading skills and to support learning across the curriculum. It is important to use clear selection criteria to ensure that the children have access to reading materials appropriate to their different reading abilities, interests and general maturity.

Texts to teach reading

Books to develop the children's reading skills must be chosen with care. You will be using books for different purposes – to teach specific reading skills, to practise and consolidate reading skills, and to foster the children's interest in books.

- Children should be able to read the book that you are using with 90–95 per cent accuracy. The aim is to promote fluent and accurate reading skills; if the child is having to hesitate and stop over too many unknown words it is an inappropriate text for specific teaching of reading.

- If the child is reading a book independently they should be able to read it with a high degree of accuracy – at least 95 per cent. If they are having to guess too many words they will become frustrated, and will also lose some or much of the meaning.

- A book for sharing with others does not demand such high levels of accuracy; 80–85 per cent is sufficient.

Many schools employ a colour-coding system to determine the reading age levels of different texts and children are guided to make appropriate choices for their reading books. *NASEN A–Z Graded List of Reading Books* (Hinson and Gains, 1997) provides a comprehensive survey of the reading levels of the most popular primary reading books.

All children will require plenty of reading practice. Children who are experiencing more difficulty in acquiring reading skills benefit from reading some texts more than once as this helps them develop fluency, speed, accuracy and confidence. Re-reading texts should not be presented in an inhibiting way but as a positive experience. You can ask the child to read their book to a friend, or to another adult (possibly taking the book home). They can tape their reading or possibly go to a class of younger children to share their story with them.

There are some children who may be developing relatively accurate reading skills but who show some reluctance about reading. With these children it is particularly important to differentiate the reading materials by taking into consideration their interests. Some children do not enjoy fiction and will respond much better to information books, poetry, books presented in different formats – picture or comic books, for example. Interactive books on CD-ROMs can act as a powerful motivator for reluctant readers.

Able readers require a breadth of reading materials to extend their reading experience and to enable them to develop higher-order reading skills. When hearing these children read, differentiate your teaching approach by your use of questioning – ask the child more allusive questions, refer to aspects of punctuation, require the child to relate their reading to other experiences and to develop a more critical literacy appreciation.

Published schemes

In primary classrooms the most commonly used published schemes are those to support the development of reading skills and mathematics.

Most, if not all, of these schemes are based on a broadly developmental framework. In other words, the skills and concepts are presented in a way that gradually increases in complexity or sophistication. For example, in reading schemes the number of words that the children have to read and the cues that they have to use to decode the words increase as they progress through the scheme.

It is possible to differentiate by pace when using these schemes, by letting children progress through the scheme at different speeds – one child may be on 'Book 2' and another on 'Book 3'. It is, however, important to assess whether this is a sufficiently sophisticated form of differentiation. Some children do not need to read every book in a scheme or complete every page in a maths scheme as they already have a secure knowledge and understanding of the concepts and skills. Religiously following the structure of the scheme will not be offering them enough challenge. These children will need resources and activities that will extend them and, possibly, to move at an accelerated rate through the scheme. Other children will find the learning steps too great – even though they may have 'done' the pages on addition, that will not necessarily mean that they understand the concept and they may require further opportunities to reinforce it.

If you are using a structured reading scheme it is necessary to have a range of supplementary reading books with the same degree of difficulty for the children who need plenty of reinforcement and rehearsal. Taking them automatically to the next book may lead to failure and frustration.

Reading materials to support learning

A variety of reading materials are used to support children's learning across all areas of the curriculum – information books, reference books, resource and worksheets, information technology (including CD-ROMs), original sources, charts and posters. Careful choice of materials and ways in which you use them can prove an effective way of differentiating.

Determining the readability

Many information books demand a high reading competence from the children. It is important to be aware of the reading age of the texts that you use and their accessibility to certain children or groups in the class. If you have concerns about a particular text, a simple solution is to show the text to a child with weaker literacy skills and ask them to read a section to you. If they read hesitantly and inaccurately, you will have to modify the text in some way before using it as a resource.

A more formal method is to use a readability formula. These formulae calculate the approximate reading age required to read a text, taking into consideration factors such as the length of sentences, the number of polysyllabic words, etc. It should be emphasised that the formulae are only an approximation – plus or minus a year in reading competence. The formulae which have been shown to be most reliable for the primary age range (Harrison, 1980) are the Mugford formula and chart, Fry graph and the Spache formula.

Certain word processing packages now include a readability formula as one of their features. If you type a section from the text the reading age required will be calculated automatically.

Introducing texts

Many of the difficulties that children encounter with information texts lie in the use of subject-specific vocabulary which they may not have met before. The children's access to the text can be supported by introducing them to some of the key words before they use the book. The introduction of the words provides opportunities for discussion and clarification. Ways of introducing specific words include:

- glossaries of the words, using simple precise meanings or picture cues for children with greater difficulty (see Chapter 7)

- glossaries which extend and challenge the more able children – this could include a list of words that the children have to research to define

- wall lists, posters, lists on the board

- individual subject dictionaries

- pre-lesson tutoring, if support staff are available.

If a group of children have particular reading difficulties, introduce the words very carefully, demonstrating how they can use certain decoding strategies to read the word, for example, breaking the word into syllables or highlighting its visual similarity with other words.

If there are some children in the class who still find the level of reading too challenging it will be necessary to provide an accessible information sheet which contains the key information found in the reference book.

Using original source material by more able children in history lessons is frequently challenging due to the less familiar language and ways of presentation. If less able children are to have access to the same information, you may have to produce a simpler version which contains the information relating to the central learning objective for that activity. The children can look at the original source material but do not have to rely on it to glean the information.

More able children should be encouraged to develop their own research skills and to use a breadth of information sources, rather than just one standard text. Introduce these children to various sources by providing them with a list of options which they may wish to use.

Example

Key Stage 2 Geography: The weather project

Information sources you may choose to use:
- reference books from school library (weather section)
- newspaper weather reports
- weather reports from radio or television (including shipping forecasts)
- CD-ROM 'Weather'
- writing to the Metereological Society.

Tick which sources you have used.
Did you use any other sources?
Write down the additional sources you used.

Ways of recording work

Recording work can present huge challenges to certain children. The children may well understand the underlying concept of the activity but be unable to demonstrate this understanding on paper. This difficulty can result in understandable frustration. Providing alternative ways of recording can also extend more able pupils as it can provide them with valuable tools for independent study. Altering the ways in which you expect the children to record is a very effective way of differentiating as the different ways will reflect the children's different abilities and strengths.

Teachers use a variety of ways for differentiating the support that they offer children with their writing. In reception classes (and classes with older children) some children write on top of the teacher's writing, others copy underneath, others may be using Breakthrough folders or words written on cards and some children may be writing some words independently and using a word book for unfamiliar words.

There should be a range of dictionaries and word lists available. Children with weaker literacy skills should have access to a picture dictionary for nouns and verbs. It is also very supportive to make a list of common irregular words readily accessible to the children. This list can be displayed in the class as a common resource or individual lists can be made for specific children. The latter approach has the advantage that the child does not have to keep looking up to copy the word – something that many children find very difficult. Another effective differentiated resource to help children with very weak literacy skills is a personalised folder of words which have pictures or symbols drawn on the cards to help the child identify the relevant word. Some children will need access to an alphabet strip to use as a model for forming their letters. It can also be used as a reference point when using dictionaries or a word book.

More able children should be introduced to more sophisticated dictionaries, and if they have a reading age of approximately 8.6 they can use a spell-checker such as the Franklin Spellmaster. Introduce the children to a thesaurus to encourage them to extend their vocabulary usage.

It is important to note that it is not always necessary for children to write a full account of their work using a traditional 'essay' structure. You should consider the purpose of the recording exercise and what the central learning objective for the activity is. In an English activity the central learning objective may well relate to accurate sentence structure, correct punctuation and the construction of a coherent passage, but if the lesson has a scientific learning objective, for example the observation of a specific change over time, a list or flow diagram might be the most appropriate recording format. Ideas for recording include:

- lists
- webs
- flow diagrams
- diagrams/pictures
- tables
- cloze procedures
- taping
- using prepared materials.

Some of these ideas are explored in more depth below.

Lists

Lists can be used in a number of ways – for describing things in sequence, for developing simple note taking and for collecting more detailed information. Three examples are given on page 52.

Differentiate by asking children to offer more or less information and by requiring some children to write full sentences (see third example) and other children one-word notes or phrases (see second example).

Web diagrams

Web diagrams are a useful way of describing things which do not require a specific sequence. Write the central theme or idea in the centre of the web and then the children write their ideas

Example 1

Key Stage 1 Design and Technology

Describe how you made your model.

1   I drew my design.
2   I got the boxes and glue.
3   I copied my design and stuck it together.
4   I painted it.

Example 2

Key Stage 1 English

Words to describe Jack (from Jack and the Beanstalk)

silly
brave
greedy
happy

Example 3

Key Stage 2 History

Write down five things you found out about Anglo Saxon houses.

1

2

3

4

5

around it. The webs can be differentiated by providing more or fewer spaces for different groups of children.

Web diagrams are also a useful way of providing additional support for children who find it difficult to generate ideas for either creative or factual writing. When a subject for writing has been given to the children, ask them to brainstorm all the ideas that they can about the subject and to record these ideas on a web. The children then think about how they can use these ideas in their work. If they have particular problems structuring their work, let them use scissors to cut out their ideas from around the web and then sort them into an appropriate order.

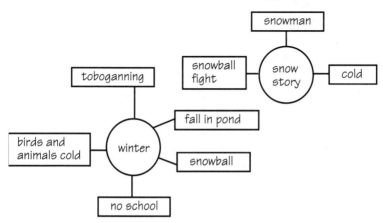

Now cut out and stick in order
1.
2.
3.
4.
5.

Flow diagrams

Flow diagrams are appropriate for recording sequential information. The information may be recorded pictorially or with words (this is another way of differentiating the activity). Children with weaker skills respond best to this activity if you have provided a specific number of boxes or spaces to fill in;

more able children have greater challenge if the task is more open-ended and they have to determine how many elements they should include. Children with very weak skills may need even greater support. This can be provided by letting them cut out prepared captions (either drawn or written) and asking them to stick these captions in the correct order.

We went outside.

He fell down.

It was snowing.

We made a snowman.

We put on warm clothes.

Diagrams/pictures

Letting children record their work pictorially is a good strategy. Although you want the children to produce work of a high standard, it is important to remember that this form of recording is not primarily an art activity – sometimes children take an inordinately long time carefully colouring work, which distracts them from the main task. Be specific about what the children are to record, emphasising the important features and discouraging irrelevant detail or elaboration.

Differentiation can be introduced by varying the amount of labelling that you require from different children or the number of specific features you want included.

Change requirements depending upon the children's abilities. Further differentiation is possible by providing some children with key vocabulary to help them label their picture.

Drawing is also a good way of introducing a written task for children who have particular difficulty organising their thoughts – drawing helps them to synthesise their ideas and this clarification is reflected in their subsequent written work. For example, if you want the children to describe the comparative design merits of two products, ask some children to sketch the two products first, emphasising the design features they like or dislike. Following the completion of their drawing, ask them to write their conclusions.

Tables and graphs

Tables and graphs offer ways of condensing information, but for children with weaker mathematical or spatial skills they can present serious difficulties. Once again you can differentiate the activity by varying the amount of information to be recorded. If the children are required to record some information on a graph and the central learning objective is not mathematical (for example, recording the rate of growth of a shoot) then it may be appropriate to provide some children with prepared axes so that they only have to record their data. Other children would be expected to prepare the graph from scratch.

Cloze procedure

Cloze procedure is a well established technique in which children are expected to complete gaps in a text with the relevant missing words. It reduces the amount of writing that they have to complete but concentrates their attention upon key words or phrases. It is important that the cloze procedures are constructed in such a way that the children have to understand the text fully, and that they cannot be completed automatically, with no comprehension.

Elements of differentiation may be introduced by varying the number of spaces that you leave for the children to complete and by providing a bank of words for some children to use while more able children have to generate or find their own words. Some children may need the extra support of dashes that indicate the number of letters in the correct word.

Example

Key Stage 1 Geography

Central learning objective – to recognise differences between two places in the UK

Group 1

Newlyn is by the _____ .

It is a small _____.

People go on _____ to Newlyn.

They catch _____ in Newlyn.

Birmingham is a big _____.

They make _____ in Birmingham.

Birmingham is a long way from the _____.

Words to help you:

town   cars   fish   holiday   city   sea

Recording children's verbal responses

Many of children's responses in school are verbal, and noting these responses is another way of providing differentiated opportunities for the children. Children have different levels of verbal skills and these can be recognised by having different expectations and/or by asking groups or individuals to undertake different tasks. It is important to remember that some children with weaker literacy skills may have well developed verbal skills and using verbal activities allows them to demonstrate their knowledge and understanding.

Ways of recognising the children's verbal responses

- If the children are working in a group nominate (or ask the group to nominate) a spokesperson who will report the outcome of the group's work to the class.

- Pair a child who is reticent or has weaker language skills either with a peer with whom they feel confident or an adult – the child can either practise what they are going to say or tell their partner what they want to say.

- Allow less confident children to make notes before they speak to the class or group.

- Let the children use tape recorders to record their ideas. (Children with weaker literacy skills may well need to develop this skill to a high level if they are going to use dictaphones or voice-activated word processors in the future.) With certain activities and for specific children it may be appropriate for the children to write down their words at a later stage; for other children you may act as a transcriber.

- In the case of pupils with more sophisticated oral skills, give clear expectations of what you want them to include in their verbal account – the number of facts, the use of specific vocabulary, the length of their account. Encourage them to refine and elaborate their report.

Integrating different methods of recording in a differentiated lesson

The examples on pages 59 and 60 show how methods of recording information can be differentiated in a Key Stage 2 Science lesson.

Example

Key Stage 2 Science

Central learning objective: Animals and plants are adapted
to their habitat

Class divided into three groups.

Group 1

Draw one animal and one plant which lives in each of these
places:

Desert

Arctic

Draw arrows to show parts of the animal and plant which help
it survive there.

Possible extension – children to write notes describing the
features they have highlighted.

Group 2

Write the name of five plants and/or animals that live in these areas.

desert	arctic	jungle
•	•	•
•	•	•
•	•	•
•	•	•
•	•	•

Why are these animals/plants suited to living in these places? Give at least three reasons.

•	•	•
•	•	•
•	•	•
•	•	•

Group 3

1   Make lists of the types of adaptations that plants and animals need to live successfully in:

   – the desert
   – the jungle.

2   Give examples of five animals/plants for each type of habitat.

3   Draw a picture of an imaginary animal that would be well suited to living in the arctic.

Differentiated worksheets

Worksheets are one of the resources used most frequently by teachers. They may be commercially produced or made by the teacher to support a particular learning objective or activity.

Published worksheets

As with any published resource, you need to ask certain questions to ascertain whether the worksheet is appropriate for your class or groups of children. These questions include:

- Does the worksheet address the central learning objective that you have determined?

- What reading level does the worksheet demand?

- Is the layout confusing or too complex for some or all of the children?

- Is it possible to complete the worksheet mechanically without true understanding?

- Is the activity 'fit for the purpose' – for example, if you want the children to learn different phonic sounds is it appropriate to use a worksheet, which is essentially a quiet working activity?

- Does the worksheet require the children to do things which could be regarded as a waste of time (for example, too much colouring)?

- What skill or conceptual level does the worksheet demand? Which groups of children would find it challenging? Would it be an appropriate consolidation activity for another group?

- How long should different children take to complete the activity? (The answer to this question would assist you to differentiate by pace – setting an expectation, for example, for one group to finish within 10 minutes and another in 20 minutes.)

The answers to these questions will tell you whether the worksheets are appropriate for all or some of the class.

Preparing your own worksheets

The questions shown above are also relevant when you produce your own worksheets. The key considerations are:

- the central learning objective
- the skill level (including the literacy skills) of the children
- the children's different levels of understanding.

In response to these issues you can differentiate the worksheets by:

- changing the reading level demanded (amount and complexity of text)
- providing specific support (e.g. use of symbols and pictures)
- changing the size of print
- changing the amount of recording required by the children
- changing some of the conceptual content
- varying the complexity of the layout
- increasing/reducing the amount of cross-referencing that the children are expected to undertake.

The example on pages 63 and 64 shows how worksheets for a single topic can be differentiated. Obviously all these worksheets would be introduced through a class discussion.

With Group 3 it would be possible to differentiate further by providing additional materials for some children (for example, a blank tally chart) or by directing them towards a particular way of recording the data or the types of vehicles that they should record.

Example

Key Stage 2 Mathematics: Data handling

Central Learning Objective – to collect and record data about frequency of different vehicles passing

---

Group 1

Traffic survey

How many do you see in 10 minutes?

cars

lorries

bikes

buses

Group 2

Use a tally chart to record the different vehicles you see in 10 minutes.

cars

lorries

vans

tankers

farm vehicles

two-wheeled vehicles

Record this information using a bar graph.

Group 3

You have to do a traffic survey.

Decide which types of vehicles you are going to look for.

Keep a tally for 10 minutes.

Decide how you will record the information. (Possible ways include a block graph and a pie graph.)

Don't forget that you can use the computer.

Using information technology to support differentiation

Information technology can be used across the curriculum to support children's different skills and weaknesses.

Word processing

One of the most obvious ways in which word processing can support children is by enhancing the quality of the presentation of their work. Some children with poor fine motor skills can be disheartened that their work, regardless of the content, looks unattractive. By providing them with the opportunity to use a word processing program you enable them to produce work of a high quality.

Remember that word processing is not simply typing out what has already been handwritten into neat copy. Such activity has little educational value. Children need to be taught how to compose directly on to the screen and how to edit their work – either on the screen or using a hard copy. This is of particular importance for children who, for whatever reason, may have to rely heavily on word processing for recording their work.

It is important that it is not only children with poor handwriting skills who have access to the computer – all children need to develop competence in word processing and it should be seen as a highly valued skill. It is necessary to analyse the task you are planning to see if word processing will reduce the burden of recording for some children.

Word processing packages are becomingly increasingly flexible. Explore the facilities of your programs to see how they can support and develop children's skills.

- Many programs allow you to build a word bank at the bottom of the screen. These can be tailor-made to specific children's needs – some children require only new subject-specific words, others need a more extensive vocabulary which includes common keywords.

pyramid camel
Egypt pharoah

- For some children a blank screen can be as daunting as a blank piece of paper. Use word processing programs which incorporate a graphic element. Draw a picture of the subject of the children's work on to the 'page'. This reduces the amount of space that the children have to fill and can have a very positive impact on more reluctant writers.

- Word processing programs that include speech facilities give children with weaker literacy skills the chance to check their work and to gain a greater independence in their work. When they write their words the computer 'reads' it back. If they have mis-spelt the word they should be able to hear it and try to correct it.

- Technology is developing very fast and it will not be long before voice-activated word processors are more generally available. These transform the children's speech into print.

- Changing the size of the print on the word processing program is a simple but effective way of differentiating the expectations that you have for the amount of written work from different children.

- Increasing the size of the print is important to children with poor literacy skills. They find large print easier to read.

- Some word processing programs allow you to change the colour of the screen. You may find that some children find different colours easier to work on.

- More able primary-aged pupils should be introduced to the spell-checking facilities of the word processing programs to increase their independence. Spell-checkers are occasionally seen as, potentially, of greatest benefit for less able pupils but a child needs quite a high reading age to be able to read the alternatives offered. Spell-checkers are also only effective for picking up errors that are reasonable spelling alternatives or typing errors – mistakes which are too bizarre may not be recognised. If you feel that a child with slightly weaker literacy skills would benefit from a spell-checker, use a word processing program with a speech facility. This lets the child hear the alternatives offered by the program.

There are some very good handheld spell-checkers which children can use when they are not using the computer. These are, again, more appropriate for children with stronger literacy skills as the children will be either able to spell the words accurately (and so they are truly checking their spelling) or will be making minimal errors.

Concept keyboards

Concept keyboards offer tremendous flexibility. The overlays can be tailor-made to meet specific learning needs.

For children with weak literacy skills concept keyboards can be used as an early introduction to word processing. For general use make overlays that include common keywords which the children will need frequently. When the children are writing about a certain topic make subject-specific overlays. These can be differentiated depending upon the levels of different children or groups.

Example

Science topic – Electricity

Words for overlay 1	**Words for overlay 2**
electricity	electricity
light	current
switch	central heating
off	fridge
on	computer
etc.	etc.

This approach can also be used to differentiate the level of support offered for children's story writing skills.

- Draw pictures (or symbols) on the overlays for children who have very weak literacy skills, or use a combination of words and pictures, if the children have begun to develop a sight vocabulary.

- Concept keyboards are useful for developing children's word-building skills. Children will have different levels of phonic understanding and competence. These can be addressed by having a bank of overlays which cover the range of phonic ability in the class. You can then match these to individual children's needs.

Example

Differentiated overlays to develop children's phonic skills

Objective: To build words in -an family

b c D f m N p t St th -an

Objective: To build words beginning with br- blend

br- ain ake anch ead eak ick ight ing

Objective: To build words with 'i' as medial vowel

i t p ll ck s b r d n

Concept keyboards can be used to differentiate activities when you require pupils to sequence events chronologically. Some children will be able to retain the order of many more elements than others and this can be reflected by the number of cells you use on the concept keyboard.

Example

History activity

Objective: Sequence Jack and the Beanstalk story in correct order (pictures used)

Overlay 1	**Overlay 2**
Mother gives Jack cow	Mother gives Jack cow
Jack swaps cow for beans	Jack goes to market
Jack plants beans	Jack swaps cow for beans
Beanstalk grows	Mother cross with Jack
Jack climbs beanstalk ...	Jack plants beans
	Beanstalk grows
	Jack looks surprised
	Jack climbs beanstalk ...

Further support can be offered by using concept keyboards with the speech facility.

Graphics programs

Some children find drawing very difficult and are often dissatisfied with their artistic attempts. Choose graphics programs which allow maximum flexibility, for example, programs which include templates which children with poor fine motor skills can incorporate in their art work. This lets them produce work that they can be proud of.

As with all such supports for learning, it is important that the children do not become too reliant upon them. You have to choose when it is appropriate to let them use the templates – in other words, when drawing is not the central focus of the activity. On occasions when you want to concentrate on developing the children's drawing skills, it would not be appropriate to let them use the program.

Other useful software which supports differentiation

- Some children need extra support to help them organise their ideas. There are some programs which provide a structured way for children to do this. The children 'brainstorm' their ideas on to the screen and the program allows them to move the ideas around the screen until they feel that they have established a coherent order. (It is possible to replicate this form of support without using a computer. Ask the children to write their ideas down on a piece of paper. When they have recorded what they feel are the most important points get them to cut out the ideas and put the pieces of paper in a logical order.)

- The use of symbols to ensure that pupils with weaker literacy or language skills gain maximum access to the lessons has already been mentioned. A symbols program such as 'Writing with Symbols' is very flexible. It can be used with concept keyboards to enable the children to write with much greater flexibility. The program can be used to prepare worksheets. Print on worksheets or tasksheets used in conjunction with symbols can enable children with poor literacy skills to take part and follow the same activity as the rest of the class. This is an excellent example of differentiation through resources.

- The multi-media programs and, in particular, CD-ROMs offer more opportunities for differentiation. Information on the CD-ROMs is presented in various forms – visually, aurally and in print. This means that you are able to guide children to the most appropriate presentation for them. CD-ROMs used as reference sources often include the information at different levels of sophistication and complexity. This gives you the opportunity to extend more able children by asking them to use a more sophisticated level.

- The facilities offered by information technology expand at an incredible rate and it is important to keep your eyes open for new developments which will assist you in differentiating the resources available for the children. One facility currently being developed is a speech-activated word processor which will type what you say. Such a program would provide another valuable support for children who have difficulty recording their work.

Differentiating the hardware

Hardware as well as software can assist you in differentiating. Children have different motor skills; this includes their hand–eye co-ordination and the accuracy of their fine motor skills. In recognition of this it is important to build up a store of different computer adjuncts.

- Very young children or those with poor hand–eye co-ordination find using a traditional mouse very difficult. For these children a trackball, particularly the very big trackball, can be the answer.

- There are now a variety of keyboards available. Some are ergonomically designed for children with very specific physical difficulties and there are also those that are extended and enlarged. Some keyboards present the letters in alphabetical order – although the utility of these keyboards should be evaluated carefully as the children will have to 'unlearn' that order when they encounter the more traditional QWERTY arrangement. It is possible to buy keyboards which use lower-case letters, which are useful to support children who do not know capital letters. A cheaper alternative to buying these keyboards is to stick lower-case letters on top of the standard keys.

Other forms of technology that offer differentiated resources

- Calculators are in frequent use in classrooms. It is important to determine the objective of the lesson to see if the use of a calculator is relevant for individual children. If the object of the lesson is to develop a fluent and accurate knowledge of number bonds it is inappropriate to offer a calculator to children who find number bonds difficult. If they have a calculator they will rely too heavily upon it and will not have the chance to learn the number bonds with the almost automatic response which you would wish. If, however, the central learning objective of the lesson is not connected with number, giving the children a calculator may remove an unnecessary burden which will allow them to concentrate on the purpose of the lesson. Providing calculators for more able pupils may be appropriate. It allows them to complete an extension activity successfully when they can understand the concepts but are unable to compute the necessary number work without the calculator.

- Tapes and cassettes are very useful pieces of equipment.

  - Commercially produced tapes that accompany stories give children access to the books and may also help develop their reading skills.

  - If you have children with very weak literacy skills in your class, taping important text books or reference materials facilitates their access to the curriculum. (It is a good idea to ask adult volunteers to record some of the most used reference materials, which you can then keep in a central store.)

  - Small dictaphones are useful for children of all abilities. Use them with children with poor organisational skills. When they undertake a certain task, encourage them to use the dictaphone to record the order in which they approach the activity.

  - Let children with poor literacy skills use dictaphones to record their work, when an aspect of writing is not the central learning objective.

  - More able children can use dictaphones as *aides mèmoire* before recording their work on paper or on the computer. It will help them develop important study skills.

- Recording children's work is another way of reducing the burden of writing for children with weak literacy skills. Looking at photographs and videos of themselves and their work is often a powerful motivator for children who find it difficult to engage with school or who have low self-esteem.

Research and study skills

All children need to be taught specific research and study skills. These include:

- using an index and contents page
- skim reading
- selecting relevant information
- taking notes.

Different children will require different levels of support to acquire and develop these skills. For example, some children may need an alphabet strip to help them use an index. Weaker children benefit from having a list of key vocabulary to help them find relevant sections, or they may have to be directed to specific pages.

Note taking is a skill which many children find difficult, they frequently copy out whole sections of text without being able to identify the key elements and essential information. Providing children with a structure for note taking helps them develop the skill – this support can be differentiated in recognition of the children's different abilities. Using a cloze procedure provides good support for weaker children, whereas a more open-ended approach is appropriate for more able children. These techniques are illustrated on page 75.

Example

Key Stage 2 Science

Group 1

Molar teeth are used for ....
Draw a molar tooth.

Canine teeth are used for ....
Draw a canine tooth.

Incisor teeth are used for ....
Draw an incisor tooth.

Group 2

Write down the names of the different types of teeth.
-
-
-

Write down three things you found out about canine teeth.
-
-
-

Conclusion

In this book a number of ways have been presented in which it is possible to differentiate in the primary classroom. As pointed out in the introduction, these approaches have always been the characteristics of good primary teaching.

Some of the ideas are simple and require, for example, the provision of an additional learning resource to extend a more able group of children or provide additional support for the children who have particular difficulties. Other approaches are more time-consuming, and it is one of the many skills of a teacher to determine whether the time investment will be 'rewarded' by an appropriate gain in children's learning.

At the heart of the approach are the assessment, planning and teaching cycle and the importance of having a clear idea of what you want the children to learn – the central learning objective. With such clarity and good assessment knowledge, it is possible to plan and teach activities which will allow all the children in your class to make the greatest progress possible.

References

Harrison C. (1980) *Readability in the Classroom*. Cambridge: Cambridge University Press.

Hinson M, Gains C. (1997) *NASEN A–Z Graded List of Reading Books*. Stafford: NASEN.